No. 156

CONCERTO

in F major

FOR PIANO

By

HELEN BOYKIN

The traditional three movements of the concerto form are effectively used in this concerto as follows:

First: ALLEGRO—a Sonata Allegro with contrasting opening and second themes developed to a stirring climax.

Second: ANDANTE — which provides a quiet interlude based upon a finely spun melody.

Third: ALLEGRO VIVACE — in which the classic rondo form is used as a brilliant finale to the Concerto.

ISBN 978-0-7935-8767-4

Associated Music Publishers, Inc.

DISTRIBUTED BY

HAL•LEONARD®
CORPORATION
7777 W. BLUEMOUND RD. P.O. BOX 13819 MILWAUKEE, WI 53213

Concerto

I

HELEN BOYKIN

II

Rondo

III

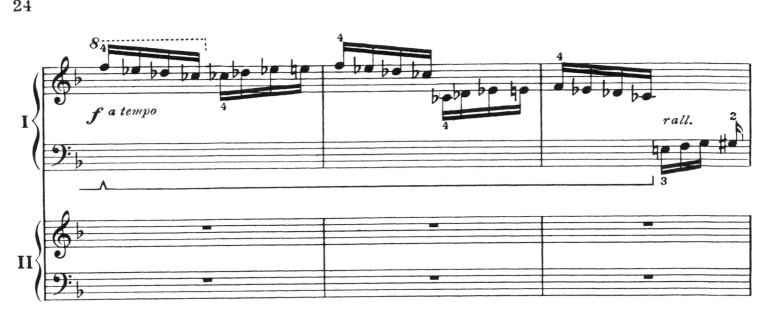

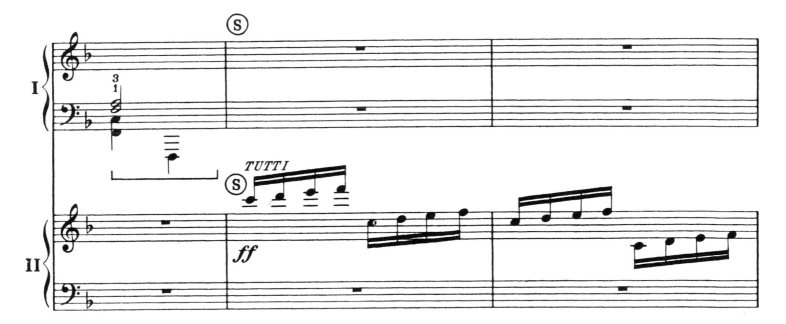